The Simple Guide to a Winning LinkedIn Profile
How to Create Your Personal Brand, Get Noticed by Recruiters, and Find That Job

By Gordon S. Worth

Copyright © 2017 by Gordon S. Worth
All rights reserved. This book or any portion thereof may not be reproduced or used in any manner whatsoever without the express written permission of the publisher except for the use of brief quotations in a book review.

Table of Contents:

Introduction

What Exactly Is LinkedIn?

Completing Your Profile

- The Photo
- Your Tagline
- The Summary
- Work Experience
- Featured Skills and Endorsements
- Education
- Volunteer Experience
- Accomplishments
- Interests
- Congruence: Bringing It All Together

How to Network

- How to Increase Your Visibility
- Things to Avoid

Conclusion

Checklist

The Simple Guide to a Winning LinkedIn Profile

Introduction

From a career development perspective, LinkedIn is by far your most important social media platform (at least in terms of conventional career avenues). Because of that, it's essential you put the time and effort into shaping it.

The contents of this book are broadly based on conversations I have within my career coaching sessions, on the LinkedIn work I do for a UK CV writing company (and based on their guidelines), and on additional observations. This is also a follow-up to my book Craft a Winning Resume, which is an essential stepping stone to presenting yourself in the most impactful way in resume form.

This book is intended to give you a solid grounding to help you set up or develop a profile that gets you noticed. Don't get sucked into thinking you need to know every single bell and whistle on the site to improve how you're perceived. You don't. Keep it simple.

Bear in mind that all forms of social media continue to evolve. What "worked" on Facebook five years ago may not be the same now. There are different algorithms, different tastes, different ways in which information is presented.

And that's the same for LinkedIn. A few years ago, writing your profile in the third person was commonplace. Now, the norm is to write it in the first person. We've also seen LinkedIn completely revamp its interface a few times. So, if you are going to keep your LinkedIn relevant, make sure you base your approach on the more up-to-date practices.

If you already have a profile, before you get moving on your LinkedIn edits, make sure you turn your activity broadcasts off – at least temporarily. This will prevent your whole network from being advised of every single simple change you make.

To do this, click on the tiny avatar of yourself in the top right of the screen. From the dropdown menu, choose **Setting & Privacy**, then **Privacy**, then **Profile Privacy** and then **Sharing Profile Edits** before turning off your activity broadcasts.

If you're starting this from scratch, welcome to the journey.

Let's begin on creating a LinkedIn profile that works.

What Exactly Is LinkedIn?

In very simple terms, it's THE social media platform for professionals. Yes, that is an incredibly simplified way of describing it, as anyone can tell you that Facebook, Twitter et al. all have a role in a business context.

But if you're looking to connect with people in your industry, get yourself known to recruiters or search for job opportunities, LinkedIn serves multiple roles. You can't expect the job hunting approach from 7 – 10 years ago to be as successful in the digital world.

Times have changed, and that's why you must become conversant with the platform.

LinkedIn is there for online networking. And that's the charm and curse of it. It's great that you've got a one-stop shop for getting yourself out there in a professional manner. But it also means that you've got to be a bit more measured on how you project yourself when compared with Facebook, for example.

This is not the place to post pictures of your bachelor party. Nor is it the place to post comments that can easily offend. What people may accept in your close Facebook network may be career suicide if you post the same item on LinkedIn.

The power of LinkedIn really comes with its reach. It's not just about your direct connections. It's also about your connections' connections. And your connections' connections' connections, and so on. In other words, you can get to engage with individuals in a manner that couldn't happen in any other way.

LinkedIn's been around since 2002, and its exponential growth in recent years simply shows how the digital world has evolved to its fundamental role nowadays. In several careers, if you're not on the platform, you don't exist!

I often hear friends say they've signed up to LinkedIn but haven't done anything with it. Think about a time you've gone to a networking event and have stood in the corner, hoping that someone would come up to you for a chat.

If you remain on the edges of the room, don't make yourself known and don't engage in any conversation, you may as well be a wall plant. Yes, someone might come up to you by chance, but you shouldn't expect it. It's the same on LinkedIn.

You can't expect to be "found" by recruiters if they don't know you exist. And a lot of this book is all about making sure people know what you're about and notice you, rather than simply being a fly on the wall.

This might feel odd and uncomfortable, but it's the world we live in. You've got to establish a presence so as to be seen in the first place.

You've also got to look at LinkedIn as a search engine. You may be the best chef known to man, but if your profile is pretty thin on information (relevant or otherwise), you can't expect anyone to know about your talents. This is about marketing yourself, and that takes a different set of skills and awareness than simply being able to do your job well.

This book is about helping you to improve how you optimize your profile, whether that's for personal branding, making new connections or being discovered by recruiters.

How should your LinkedIn compare with your resume?

A great metaphor I once heard suggested that LinkedIn is the equivalent of "smart casual," while your resume is "formal wear." LinkedIn gives you scope to show a bit of personality and a bit of charm. You still have to present yourself in the right way, but it's not as strict as your resume.

As I will keep reinforcing throughout this book, your LinkedIn is also a living, breathing document that is there to be viewed by anyone all the time, and as a result, it should/can be amended by you regularly to stay relevant. You can't just write it and leave (as you would more likely do with a resume). You've got to view it as an ongoing narrative with a wide global online audience, rather than something you simply set and forget.

Completing Your Profile

If you already have a profile, great. This book should help you improve what you already have. Before diving into any changes, make sure you adjust your privacy settings. This is so you do not tell the whole world what you are doing.

Click on **Settings & Privacy** from the menu. Select Privacy. Scroll to **Sharing Profile Edits** and switch to **No**. This prevents others from seeing you are updating your profile. This is especially important if you don't want your boss to become aware of the updates.

Select **Who Can See Your Connections**, then select **Only You**. This protects you from others viewing your connections. Change this setting to this if you are using LinkedIn for job-hunting purposes.

Next, it's important to personalize your public profile. You want to make sure what people see is what you want to represent.

Select **Profile**, then **Edit Profile**. Find the public URL link under your profile photo and click on the cog when it appears.

If this is all new to you, welcome! Try and keep up as we go through how the site operates.

The Photo

Social media is full of "lurkers" – people who sign up to a platform and spend most of their time looking at other people's profiles and information. And that's fine. This is not a judgement call.

But for LinkedIn, it doesn't add any value to be shy. That's because it's reason of being is for connection and engagement on a platform where business prospects, professional acquaintances or future employers can find you.

So, it's important to get yourself out there.

This starts with your picture. Research (I think from LinkedIn) indicates that profiles with a picture are 14 times more likely to be viewed than those without.

It stands to reason. If you don't have a picture at all there's simply more reason for someone not to trust you.

After all, there are plenty of scam artists online trying to contact you via LinkedIn. If there's no face to the name, you do wonder whether this is a real person or not.

For your photo, make sure you are in professional attire (whatever that represents for you in your industry), have a clean background and are well groomed. It's all about giving off the right impression to potential clients, employers and headhunters. I always recommend a simple head and shoulders shot with a neutral background and a warm expression.

It's a 500 x 500 pixel image, so factor that in and make sure you are looking forward or left – it's a standard.

What you don't want to do is throw in a selfie or a photo that shows the cropped arm of your colleague. You can also name your headshot (yourname.jpg) and upload it. That picture now reflects "you."

If you really want to take it to the next level, put your photos through photofeeler.com. This site tells you exactly how you're being perceived in your photos so you can choose the one that makes the most sense for LinkedIn.

And remember to refresh your profile photo occasionally. This will help boost the views. According to data from LinkedIn, Millennials change their photo more frequently than any other age group. This also means they're the most viewed demographic on the site.

This is no different to Facebook – you get more attention when you change your profile picture. No need to go overboard, but think about it in the context of a broader strategy to attract more attention to your profile.

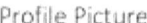

Profile Picture

The difference here is your picture on LinkedIn must be professional, or at least it cannot be viewed as unprofessional. Once again, the picture you provide projects your personal brand, so keep that in mind when you post a photo.

Let's go next to:

Your Tagline

This is one of the most overlooked parts of a profile. Aside from your photo, it's the first introduction you make to the LinkedIn world. There are a few different ways you can play these 120 characters (which is all you get). But the important thing is to say something. If you leave it blank, you really don't give people a reason to click onto your full profile.

LinkedIn automatically makes the headline that appears below your name your current job title and employer. And that's what most people stick with. It's better than leaving it bare but you should think about being more creative.

For example, if you are an account manager who has written a book and has done talks at seminars, compare the following:

- Account Manager
- Account Manager | Author | Speaker | I build multinational media brands

Same person, different personal brands. Actually, the first person could be an entirely different person – it's very generic and doesn't tell the reader much about what else you have to offer. So always keep in mind what you want the reader to know about you.

LinkedIn weighs the headline relatively heavily in terms of search engine optimization (SEO). So, if someone was looking for "account manager" and "multinational," your profile would likely appear higher in the rankings than simply "account manager."

Remember, LinkedIn works as a search engine, so it's important to liberally sprinkle the right keywords across your profile, including in the tagline.

If you want a recruiter to discover you as someone who's great at graphic design, as well as an expert in caricature, you can literally put "Graphic Designer and Caricaturist." That way, there's an increased chance your face could pop up if someone keys in these phrases.

Like above, you could expand on that. How about "Graphic Designer | Caricaturist | works with ceramics"? If that better sums you up, then great. It throws in another keyword in "ceramics" and allows you to use up a bit more of your characters quota.

How do you find the right keywords? Some of it is intuitive. Think about the words that a recruiter would use. But if you need additional help, LinkedIn offers its own profile optimization/writing service, **LinkedIn Profile Writing Service**. Search for it on the platform for tips and tricks.

What if you're not currently in gainful employment but are hunting?

If you are looking for a new role, there's nothing wrong with putting "seeking new opportunity." Some people feel a bit embarrassed to say they are job hunting so they don't like to put anything there.

The trouble with that is, of course, if you don't let people know your current status, how will they know whether to reach out to you?

An alternative approach would be to say you are "on sabbatical," which can often be interpreted as taking a break but open to conversations.

The Summary

This is the most important part of your LinkedIn. You have 2000 characters to show what you're about.

It's vital you have something engaging here. It's your Summary that will engage recruiters first. Here, you are telling a story, which includes giving a sense of your passions, and even anecdotes to get your message across. Make sure you talk about yourself in the first person.

Research shows that users who have at least 40 words in their summary section tend to be able to drive more page views, which can enable more search results, particularly if you use a good selection of keywords.

In your summary, spell out your strengths and experiences that align with the core deliverables of the types of jobs you're pursuing. How can you tell which ones are most important? Find three or four job descriptions that seem interesting to you and see what the most common requirements are.

This will also indicate what keywords to use – the type of words that recruiters and the like would key in when looking for a certain type of person.

And what type of wording should you use less of? Avoid waffle and be restrained in your use of certain words that have become overused: for example, "motivated," "passionate," "driven" and "responsible."

Imagine every new graduate with little in the way of experience happily throwing these words into their LinkedIn descriptions. The trouble is, these words in themselves say little about you. If you are "responsible," demonstrate exactly how you have been responsible. Does that mean you were responsible for your church fair or for a team of 20? Details are relevant.

Remember that LinkedIn is all about letting your (professional) personality shine through. It's your calling card.

So, don't be boring. Don't just talk about how many years of experience you have. There are plenty of other profiles doing that.

Sell yourself in a manner that suggests you've got something interesting to say. This is about where you show your beliefs, motivations, or values and you can show an outsider a lot more about you than simply your experience. But you have also got to be less stilted and more conversational (within reason).

Start the summary with a strong opening gambit and weave a narrative that keeps people interested. Remember: your summary is a great way to get attention, particularly if you can throw in numbers and data to make it more compelling.

The counter balance to using trite words is the idea of incorporating keywords to boost your SEO and help you become found on LinkedIn and your LinkedIn profile found by search engines.

Some headhunters do searches based on keywords, some don't. Regardless, consider the ideal person your profile would speak to and what words would make you stand out to them. Have these words thought out and ready when you create or edit your profile.

The more you use these kinds of words (without the narrative coming across as boring and stodgy), the better. For example, if you are an investment analyst, make sure you use words like "analysis," "research" and "stocks"/"bonds"/"funds" etc. Consistent use of the right keywords will get you a higher ranking when people search on LinkedIn.

Areas to incorporate great keywords include your headline, summary, interests, job titles, job descriptions and skills.

One good tool for checking on how successful your keyword selection is Jobscan. This site will allow you to analyze how well your resume/profile matches a job description.

If you struggle to know what to say, below are some summary approaches. The first one is one I've done for a client; the other ones are templates found online for general guidance. These approaches aren't for everyone, even if some headhunters are impressed by the tone. But you can adapt them for your purposes. Note: for your actual LinkedIn, they should be in normal font.

A summary I have done for a client:

Having taken a planned break, I am eager to resume my career and take on new and exciting challenges.

I have been a successful investment analyst with more than eight years' experience in building a research platform, servicing institutional client needs and delivering high-quality research for global financial organizations. Prior to that, I spent more than four years travelling around Europe as an internal auditor, combining in-depth technical expertise with a deep understanding of the drivers and objectives of international business operations.

Not only did these roles provide me with incredible opportunities to grow, they have also helped shape my vision for the next stage in my career. The skills I picked up and the insights gifted are priceless.

I am keen to apply my finance skills, cross-cultural experiences, senior-level network and proficiency in four languages to help organizations looking to build a presence in Madrid or seeking to grow their business across Europe. But equally as important, I want to be associated with an organization with principles I value, be part of a team with high aspirations, and be inspired by a culture that represents something meaningful.

Feel free to connect with me on LinkedIn if you are looking for assistance in servicing your investment analytical needs.

OPERATIONAL LEADERSHIP

♦ Project-managed and built European credit research platform from scratch for asset management firm to meet needs of traders and clients.

♦ Hired, trained and continuously improved performance of credit research teams, including managing the learning needs of UK and US resources.

SENIOR STAKEHOLDER ENGAGEMENT

♦ Mobilized a diverse range of stakeholders to achieve positive outcomes; engaged with management across a wide cultural range with different operating practices.

♦ Exhibited a high degree of experience in reviewing company processes and presenting analytical insights and opinions to business leaders.

Key Areas of Expertise: Cultural Adaptability, Business Building, Leadership, International, Performing Arts, Client Relationship Management, Investments, Finance, Social Causes, Research, Entrepreneurial, Investment Analysis,

Company Analysis, Auditing, Research, Results-Oriented, Professional Network, Non-profit Consulting

For this summary

- I first gave a general overview of what the person had done, skills they had to offer and what they were hoping to get out of being on LinkedIn.
- That was followed by some of their functional skills and examples of what they had achieved.
- There is a call to action, i.e., a request for others to reach out to the individual.
- Finally, there was a breakdown of areas of expertise with keywords.

This is a simple approach that anyone can apply.

Courtesy of the website *The Muse*, below are some other templates that can be considered.

Mission-Based Summary Template:

We all have a story. Some better than others. Built if you want to put across a personal brand that is "bigger than you," think about one that elevates you above the noise and impacts your audience.

And I am the conduit between brand and consumer.

I help clients find the subject and medium that best fits their unique identity, and then I produce high-quality content that meets their objectives.

Currently, I am a content strategist at Alliance Media, where I've collaborated with companies such as Tiffany & Co., Burger King, and Netflix.

My specialties include digital media, consumer behavior, brand awareness, and omni-channel marketing campaigns.

The Personality Summary Template:

When I was 21, I climbed Mount Everest. Not metaphorically—I literally climbed the highest mountain on Earth.

While I was hiking, I thought about quitting approximately 5,000 times. (And that's a lowball estimate.) But despite the high winds, low altitude, mental and physical fatigue, and trail mix overdose, I kept going. I'm that person. Once I say I'll do something, it will happen.

Now, I put that perseverance to work as a senior account manager for Polar. I don't have to climb any mountains...but I do have to move them.

I'm well-versed in negotiations, planning and development, relationship management, operations, and logistics coordination and scheduling.

If you're interested in grabbing coffee and talking shop (or to hear how I almost fell off the mountain at 27K feet), please send an email my way.

Work Experience

Under the Work Experience section, it's best to limit the number of different roles to six. Too many will diffuse your message. If you've had more than that number over the years, be selective and strategic. Think about what roles reflect the personal brand you want to put across. Consider roles that have the relevant keywords to be "discovered" on LinkedIn.

For example, if you want to be a Marketing Manager but two of your eight roles were as a Dance Instructor, you've got to weigh up whether your talent for ballet is the narrative you want to put across in this section. You can always include your dance role under the 'Accomplishments' section.

Turning to the meat of your Work Experience, as with your resume/CV include:

- Challenge: e.g. "I managed a team of 20 and we were set a sales target of $20m."

- Action: "I revised and refocused our sales strategy to focus more on local offices."

- Result: "The team beat its sales target by $3m thanks to the initiatives."

In principle though you are putting down the job titles, company names and dates of work that are consistent with what you have on your resume.

If you really want to jazz things up, the Description box beneath each job role has plenty of space for sharing a case study, customer testimonial or other big wins you scored at each job.

Make sure it's formatted cleanly and that it sells you and isn't just a chronological list of data.

DO NOT JUST COPY-PASTE YOUR RESUME/CV. The goal is to give the reader a sense of what you're about but doesn't have to have everything. Imagine someone finds you on LinkedIn and then asks that you send your resume/CV. There's absolutely no point in it being the exact same information.

From a pure formatting perspective, LinkedIn doesn't support Microsoft Word so it's less easy to generate standard bullet points. But a bullet point approach is still the preferred way of detailing information. Simply copy-paste a few symbols from a Word document directly onto the site.

As with all forms of social media, it's more than just the text. In your Summary and Experience sections think about uploading photos, links, videos and presentations. That won't work for everyone but visual content will certainly help you stand out against the reams of plain text profiles, especially if you're focused on an industry not known for its visuals.

Featured Skills and Endorsements

So you want to be viewed as an expert. How about outlining what you're good at and then getting some social proof? That's basically what this section is for.

You can note down up to 50 skills you have to offer. Again, from a keyword perspective it's great to load up on the skills that a recruiter would be looking for.

Be warned though. If you look around LinkedIn you'll see people with 15, 20, 30 and more skills and expertise endorsed within their profile. There's no consistent approach.

But if you want you to target the full quota of 50 skills the risk is that it can make your profile look messy and also suggest that you're a generalist rather than the specialist you are wanting to project. Keep that in mind and consider deleting skills that detract from your focus.

In order to get the most out of this section, see whether you can get recommendations and skills endorsements. This may mean reaching out to your friends and contacts and politely asking them for their assistance.

On the endorsements front sometimes it's a game of reciprocity - someone says you're good at something and gives you an endorsement, and you say they're good at something in return. It's a good visual aid for someone skimming your profile that wants to see what others think you're good at.

Recommendations are far more powerful than endorsements (it's not quite the same but it's a little like the difference between a "Like" and a thoughtful comment made on your Facebook profile). Social proof is a huge thing in the online world. Sometimes the only way you can get outsiders to trust that you can do what you say you can is for others to indicate that.

To be honest, not everyone understands what the skills endorsements are for anyway. But if you can get an ex-colleague or client to provide a recommendation, that can be a big positive.

Education

Research has shown that completing the 'Education' section of your profile drives 10 times more views than profiles without it.

So, it's important to fill out this section. If anything, it's a networking opportunity with alumni from any institution you studied at. Take this opportunity to outline your degrees, certifications and qualifications. Again, it shows your expertise.

If you don't want to "age" yourself, think about omitting the dates you attended the institution. We may be in a more accepting work environment than previous decade, but age discrimination still exists. If that is a concern for you, you don't have to offer up all the information.

Volunteer Experience

It's not just about your work accomplishments

Anyone can copy-paste their jobs-spec into LinkedIn. It only tells a potential recruiter one dynamic about you.

But what about outside of your work?

Are you a charity volunteer? Are you a member of an association? These kinds of things can go down well with hiring managers. They certainly don't want to be looking to employ one-dimensional robots.

Again, don't be shy. If you've done it and it shows a different and relevant side to you put it down. If you can incorporate good keywords here, even better.

This type of information is even more important for those looking at changing career and those with little work experience.

Accomplishments

LinkedIn allows you to list a range of other elements that are generally relevant to your professional life. The key is that you get the chance to show the depth of your knowledge and skillset in a way that perhaps you can't on your resume.

It also gives readers another chance to find common ground (e.g. a mutual ability to speak fluent Swahili). And, of course, don't forget that it gives you another opportunity to throw in useful keywords!

The extra sections are:

- Certifications (Useful for listing CPD/external professional training)
- Course (Useful for listing professional **in-house** training)
- Honor and Award
- Language
- Patent
- Project
- Publication
- Test Score

- Organization (Professional Memberships)

Interests

One thing that LinkedIn does very well is to encourage like-minded individuals to batch together in groups to advance their discussions. This could be everything from lawyers, job seekers, surveyors, hedge fund managers, university alumni, dance instructors…You name it, there's very possibly a group already there. And if there isn't, you can set one up from scratch.

It also helps you to follow influential individuals, like, say Richard Branson.

Groups are an excellent way in which to interact with others based on location, discipline, industry and so on. They help expand your reach and allow you to get heard by a captive market.

You can join up to 100 groups, and it makes sense to join as many as you feel comfortable with, simply to expand your reach but also to be in conversation with people you genuinely want to. Within each group you will able to make comments and offer articles.

Make the most of this – interaction is fundamental to getting the most out of LinkedIn. That's why you need to join those groups.

One tip is to go to the search menu and key in "LinkedIn Events Forum." This gets you access to people organizing events and forums around the world. So, if you want to get back to offline networking, this is one way of doing it.

You can find events that interest y0ou and see people who will be attending.

How do you know what kind of thing you should put down as interests? How about looking around at what others have on their profiles?

It's all about the concept of "personal benchmarking." All you need is to search LinkedIn for those that have a similar role to you at other firms in your sector. Look at what they have and see what areas you differ or overlap.

This counts for all sections of your LinkedIn profile If there are any areas that are confidently different, have a look at whether this might be a personal development opportunity.

If you are looking to target a specific company for a role, look at their LinkedIn company page. This will give you a real sense of the types of people that work for the firm, and the qualities required. On a very basic level, you can also check to see whether your skills are aligned with the skills that they highlight. This counts for both existing and former staff. You should also think about following the company as well.

Remember that unlike a company's website (which will tend to stay broadly consistent aside from the occasional news release) the LinkedIn profile is a living, breathing page that will constantly change (or at least should).

In other words, the information is far less likely to remain static because it's incredibly easy for a social media department to update. Make sure you keep abreast of any new insights that could be of use when you choose to connect with the company.

You can also get a sense of whether the company has any ongoing key initiatives that it wants to tell the world, and you may also get a sense of trends there. Is the firm actually growing, for example?

This also goes for your broader network – at any one time, one of your contacts could be making changes to his or her profile, so make it a goal to stay on top of LinkedIn news flow.

Remember this is all about networking. Look at where you have a network elsewhere and add them to LinkedIn. That could mean importing your address book contacts held in your Gmail account, for example. Add descriptive tags to your connections' profiles. That way you can easily identify people with specific expertise.

The more of your profile that is completed, the better.

Congruence: Bringing It All Together

Ok, you've sorted out your LinkedIn profile and it looks very dynamic. But is it properly aligned with your CV or resume?

Make sure you cross-check your facts and timelines. Serious discrepancies can cost you that killer job.

It's not just about the information. It's also the tone. There's no point in coming across as a Senior Executive on LinkedIn but as a Junior Associate on your resume.

Ensure that the two are equally strong and coherently put together. As mentioned earlier, your LinkedIn should also be more than a straight copy-paste of your resume as well. This is your personal branding.

With that in mind, recruiters may also look to see what well-known business people and associations you follow, in addition to trends you are following. They can do this by looking at the drop-down menu and choosing the **View recent activity** option.

If you don't set your settings to private, they'll be able to see what types of content you've shared and liked. Make sure you play the game by liking quality.

Don't forget to claim a vanity URL. For this, you essentially tailor the URL on the site to one that includes your name and isn't the generic default one. That way you can include it on your resume or any other place online that you want recruiters to click on to redirect them to your LinkedIn profile.

How to Network

LinkedIn is all about networking. As a result, you must make sure you are regularly engaged with it.

There are several ways in which you can keep yourself relevant. Importantly, you should think about ways in which to not only "get found" but also to reach out to others.

Look at the "How You're Connected" tool to see the connections of people you're connected with. In other words, there may be people in their network that you feel you would like to know.

This is a way of getting a foot in the door with decision makers by association. But don't stalk. This is meant to be a mutually beneficial interaction. Try to connect with other professionals in similar industries, with similar interests and with the competencies or connections you are looking to target.

Don't forget your alumni and former employers. Joining their groups or associations will provide you with an expanded profile that has brings a common connection.

There are several tools out there that could be useful for building both a following and contacts from a professional perspective. These include:

- **Five Hundred Plus**, an application that uses LinkedIn to help you make the most of your most valuable connections. It helps you track when you were last in touch with someone and when you should get back in touch so they don't forget you.

- **Rapportive**, which is a plugin that Shows LinkedIn profiles in your Gmail.

- **Crystal**, a standalone app as well as its Chrome extension that allows you to profile LinkedIn users profiles to detect their personality. It suggests the best ways to communicate with them.

- **Email Hunter**, an app that helps you find your prospect's email addresses. When it comes to LinkedIn, the Chrome Extension gives you a button to quickly match the profile's first name, last name and the company name with emails in their database for match.

- **Discover.ly**. Each time you visit someone's LinkedIn profile, Discover.ly can tell you if you have any mutual Facebook friends. Plus, it reveals the person's recent tweets to help you build their profile.

- **Weave Networking**, a mobile app that helps you expand your professional network. Its developer describes it as LinkedIn meets Tinder (minus the dating). Connect it to your LinkedIn profile and align with like-minded individuals from your area, industry etc.

If you have a website, you can also drive relevant traffic to it using tools that support LinkedIn Group functionality (e.g., SocialMotus, Hootsuite and Oktopost).

How to Increase Your Visibility

Now that you have your brand-new profile, you've got to make it work. It's not a "set and forget" one-time thing. You must actively manage it.

Just because you have written your profile, it doesn't mean you should sit back and wait for it to work. It's an active document that can (and should) be updated on a regular basis.

If you've just completed a course that you feel is relevant, note it down. If you feel your picture is a bit out of date, change it. And, obviously, if you shift jobs, don't forget to update your profile to reflect this.

It's easy to let your LinkedIn profile lapse over time if you only see it as a social media thing rather than as a living representation of your professional self.

Actions you can take to keep your profile noticed:

Acknowledge Content

If you're not yet ready to write a full-blown opinion piece espousing your view on third-world hunger, a simple process that will show you are still engaged in the platform is to either comment on or "Like" someone else's post, or circulate an article that is of interest to you.

It may not get you as much exposure as curating your own piece, but your activity will keep you current amongst your connections. And that's the whole point: to let others know that you still exist, what you stand for and what narrative you want to be associated with.

Reach out

If you really want to make the most of LinkedIn, you must go to the next stage, which is to be an active searcher.

This is the way to find leads, make connections and build up your own relational database. By being strategic, you can identify and collate a list of prospective managers in the hiring cycle

This isn't about cyberstalking. It's simply about reaching out to specific individuals where a mutually beneficial relationship can develop. They may be looking to fill a role, and you're the person to fill it!

Remember that companies would much rather find individuals using sites like LinkedIn rather than pay big bucks to a third-party recruiter to find you. That recruiter is very likely to trawl for candidates in LinkedIn anyway, so it's a great way to cut out the middle man.

So, look at this as a way of being targeted in your connections building. You can filter by geography, title, industry, discipline and so on to connect with the exact types of individuals that you need.

Writing

Another way of getting yourself noticed is through your writing.

Your writing shows you are an authority, or at least know a little more than the person reading your comment. You can brand yourself as a "thought leader" and see what traction you get.

You can start this by simply publishing blog posts from your LinkedIn page discussing themes in your industry, making sure it is "search-friendly" by putting in popular search terms.

Obviously, you've got to feel comfortable receiving commentary/criticism from complete strangers (not something you would normally expect from friends on Facebook, for example). But it could create a huge amount of value in an era where social media sharing is the norm.

If you feel comfortable with that maybe you can think about providing links to SlideShare presentations you've created.

Optimize your LinkedIn Profile

To get the right keywords, look at job postings that are aligned with the type of role you are looking for. The means going beyond the broad terminologies that could be applied universally across industries.

Capture the relevant technical terms for your industry. So rather than just "marketing," consider "digital marketing," "social media marketing" or whatever phrase captures more specifically what you're looking for.

Things to Avoid

There are plenty of obvious things you should consider when using LinkedIn. I can't stress enough how important the tone is – for example, the club night you attended at the weekend works wonders for your Facebook reputation but has no place on this site. LinkedIn's social, but not that social.

Here are a few others that I thought I would throw in, partly based on experience and partly based on discussions with headhunters in Hong Kong and the UK.

You can sell but not the minute you connect with them

It's just not nice. It normally happens with people you don't know but have somehow tracked down your details on LinkedIn. There's nothing wrong with reaching out to offer your employment services to an individual in a position of authority. But don't pitch a retirement plan or premium networking service for them to buy.

Be transparent. Don't try to connect with someone as a way to connect with someone you are actually interested in

No one likes to be used. Admittedly, earlier on I mentioned that you should use the connections of your connections. But you should also look at it all as relationship building.

If the first thing you do is to use them to get to someone else, it just comes across as rude and defeats the object of you wanting to be their "network friend" in the first place.

Don't try to connect with those you hated in a previous life

Maybe you've changed. Maybe they have. But think it through first.

If you try to connect with someone who you bullied at school, it will simply suggest you're someone that is willing to do anything to take advantage of networking opportunities.

Please don't "Like" every single little thing that gets posted

Think before you "Like." It's fine to show appreciation for different news articles that are posted, as long as you're doing it with the right intentions.

There's no need to be an expert writer on everything

Yes, you want to raise your profile by being viewed as a "knowledge champion" or whatever the relevant buzzword is. But in simple terms it's down to quality over quantity. I've seen a lot of dross on LinkedIn, simply because people feel the need to keep posting. Don't.

Think about how it makes you feel when you see loads of mindless, low value updates on Facebook from the same individual. Not great.

Conclusion

The fact that you've got to this part in the book suggests you've taken onboard the importance of LinkedIn in your personal branding. The best thing about that is that you're going to be streets ahead of many who simply haven't paid enough attention to the platform.

LinkedIn is such an important tool for improving your career and business prospects. Used wisely, it can raise your profile and allow your personal brand to reach a far wider audience. Used poorly, it can have a detrimental effect.

Look at how your existing profile and see whether the information in this book can help you improve on what you already have. Importantly, if you do have a specific job in mind, search out the profiles of individuals already doing the job you want. At the very least this should give you an idea of keywords to use in your profile that are directly relevant to the role (as opposed to words you think are relevant to the role).

Remember, LinkedIn will continue to evolve and it's important that you remain abreast of how those changes impact how you project yourself and how opportunities can more easily come your way.

Don't forget to align your LinkedIn with your resume. For tips on how to build a powerful resume for your personal brand, read Craft a Winning Resume.

Checklist

We've all heard the stories about the young Hollywood starlets that were in the right place at the right time to get that breakout role. You would have also read about the equally talented actresses that haven't had the lucky break and still wait tables while hoping to be discovered.

Ok, maybe the illustration isn't the most relevant, but think of LinkedIn as being a great place to get discovered by the hiring manager.

You've got to be somewhere where you can be found. Just because you have the right skills, it doesn't mean anyone will know you exist.

Simply by applying some very basic approaches from the checklist below, you will increase your chances of being found.

- **Complete your profile**: Research by LinkedIn has shown that users with complete profiles are 40x more likely to receive attention.

    By making it clear what you're about and what you are targeting, you will elevate yourself above a significant percentage of LinkedIn users.

    Don't forget to claim your LinkedIn vanity URL, and make sure the account setting is "public" once the changes are made.

- **What is a recruiter looking for?:** You've got to start to think like a recruiter. What would they want from a candidate for the type of job I'm looking for? How can I show that I have the right skills and qualities? Essentially, you've got to reverse engineer the process to deliver what the recruiters are looking for.

On a very basic level, it's everything that we're talking about throughout this book. Make sure the photo represents where you want to be, sell yourself in the right way and ensure you have the right keywords throughout your profile.

The fundamental point here is to put yourself into the shoes of others rather than simply telling the world what you want to say.

- **Be clear**: This dovetails with the previous points. If you put everything down and the reader isn't sure what you have to offer or what you're hoping to get out of it, you've missed a trick.

    You need to help the reader connect the dots. In other words, you need to let them know "this is what I do and this how I can help you." Too much of the other stuff will simply lose your audience.

- **Headshot**: I rarely click on a profile that doesn't have a photo. It either tells me it's a dead account or the person could be a scammer. So make sure you have a photo.

    If you want, you can go to a studio to get it done professionally. Alternatively, you can get a nice one done on your smartphone. Regardless, keep it clean and crisp—a headshot with no drama attached…unless drama is the personal brand you want to put across, then go for it!

- **Get your skills down**: Sometimes you simply need to spell out what you have to offer. You can note down up to 50 skills, but you don't have to fill up the full 50.

  If you start out with "Investment Strategy" and "Fund Management," but then drift into "Microsoft Word," you are kind of diluting your message. So be selective here and note them down in order of relevance.

- **Location**: If we're going to be talking about getting found, we may as well talk about location. This is a difficult one for some.

  Suppose you live in Madrid but you want to work in London. A recruiter with a job in the city will be doing his search on "London" rather than "Madrid." So ideally, you should put down the place you want to be rather than where you are.

  This isn't ideal for many people, but you've always got to keep in mind how people search rather than what you would prefer to put down for yourself.

In addition to this and Craft a Winning Resume, keep an eye out for future books to support you in your job hunting and personal branding goals.

www.ingramcontent.com/pod-product-compliance
Lightning Source LLC
Chambersburg PA
CBHW030518220526
45464CB00006B/2858